I, Menagerie

poems by

Garrett Ray Harriman

Finishing Line Press
Georgetown, Kentucky

I, Menagerie

Copyright © 2021 by Garrett Ray Harriman
ISBN 978-1-64662-476-8 First Edition
All rights reserved under International and Pan-American Copyright Conventions. No part of this book may be reproduced in any manner whatsoever without written permission from the publisher, except in the case of brief quotations embodied in critical articles and reviews.

ACKNOWLEDGMENTS

Several poems in this chapbook originally appeared in the following publications, sometimes in earlier forms:

"It is a pleasure," "Like the hummingbird" ~ *Atlas Poetica*
"Snake in the Grass" ~ *Naugatuck River Review*
Semi-Finalist in the 11th Narrative Poetry Contest (January 2020)
"The Spider Poem Remembered" ~ *Toasted Cheese Literary Journal*
"Tiger in Pastel" ~ *Kestrel*

My thanks to: Isabelle Pasquettaz, for her singular cover artwork and digital collage skills; Michael Francisco, for his exceptional "Saber" photographs at the Denver Museum; and Feby Syam Putra Ananda Hadi, for his dashing, Victorian-era titles.

Immeasurable thanks to Kevin Maines, Christen Kincaid, and the full publishing team at Finishing Line Press for giving *I, Menagerie* a chance and a spine.

And to the many editors and judges who first slushed, considered, and accepted my work: Thank you.

Publisher: Leah Huete de Maines
Editor: Christen Kincaid
Cover Art and Design: Isabelle Pasquettaz
Author Photo: Courtesy of the author
Page 30: Michael Francisco

Order online: www.finishinglinepress.com
also available on amazon.com

Author inquiries and mail orders:
Finishing Line Press
PO Box 1626
Georgetown, Kentucky 40324
USA

Table of Contents

Snake in the Grass 1

Sonnet with Owl 3

Elephant Ride, 1993 4

Thoughts on Two Fish 5

Exit the Lizard 7

Tiger in Pastel 8

Tanka with Birds 10

Rondeau with Sheep 11

The Memory of Dogs 12

Vulnerable Species 14

Wolverine in Four Figures 16

Deerly Departed 21

Tanka With Horse, Beaver & Elk 23

The Spider Poem Remembered 24

My Sister's Breasts: A Cryptozoological Interview 25

Pantoum with Raccoon 27

Smilodon Song 29

For my family, untamable

Well, it's true
We do not live in a zoo
But Man is an animal, too.
            "Like Animals"
            Dr. Dolittle, 1967

SNAKE IN THE GRASS

Because there were neighbor girls
who played night volleyball
in the backfield connecting our houses;
because we had outdoor cats;
because monsters need killing
and every American family deserves its myth,
my father hastened for my mother
to the bull snake's den,
that coiled coolness, that summer blight,
accountant's hands gloved and beshoveled.

>It was too hot to hear the slaughter,
the bramble at our fence line too thick to discern
the deed. The rank woodedness
of mid-July could only sieve gruesome thoughts
through the mothy screen door,
the imagined aftermath and carcass-lobbing
washing over our siblings' vigil
for that frenzied father's return.

Disappointment—no blood on the implement;
a rock was required to part the hydra from its head,
plus the assurance of the creature's size
and life-stubbornness,
the promise its body had been disposed of
for the bears and scavengers of the mountain.
This from our daddy dialed death merchant
for twenty minutes in a clearing
coliseumed by pines,
his civility renewed, his tutored hands clean.

> Conniptions of carnage, *coups de grâce*—
> both take such pale convincing
> if the day is hot enough. If the words are sweet.
> What skins shed the mob with virginal verve
> when the lurking largeness of a life unlived
> fangs the heart, constricts us at the start
> of any moment
> of any day...

The neighbor girls bapped and bounced
their sport through the evening:
I watched the serpent's head spinning and spiked,
served and received,
forked tongue flailing in the breeze,
eyes alive with the sins of my father,
yellow as the weeds they would become.

SONNET WITH OWL

> *Ah wretch! said they, the bird to slay,*
> *that made the breeze to blow!*
>   —*"Rime of the Ancient Mariner"*

He tells me growing up the family land
wasn't land the way you'd think, but a mound
too sacred to tamp: a bone-infused ground.
How night and day the owls circled to land,

smothering their woods in wings a thousand
deep. *"They'd watch and shade the house…"* Astounded,
he knew instinctively why—to rebound
the animus below—when, gun in hand,

his brute father stormed the porch line, took aim
from the midday sun, and fired. Long-ears
and Barns and Eastern Screeches dropped in chains;
their fogs, unblinking, evanesced like rain.

He warns me the owls' drought strengthens by years.
How it starves luck off those who share your name.

ELEPHANT RIDE, 1993

Coloring pages won
me it, the contest judged
by clowns; memories—
one of the earliest.
Rope ladder dangling
down the beast's umber flank;
updrawn by driver
into humid howdah,
carpet-draped. Slow,
massive swellings; bent
metronome gait. Muscle
gyrations—fleshy surf lapping
my feet, the air and world
one great, sloppy listing.
Dust rising from graveled
parking lot; log-round legs
upsetting rural earth—
domesticated tremors,
Attila-esque thrills.
Long, windless acres
to every compass point
                    then
                      down
again; perspective ingrained.
The pendulous pachyderm's
brown eye ticking
ten stories atop my head—
vitreous, weary—watching
me go till this moment; till
this servitude of words
be spoken,
peace-broken. Tent rolled
and posts upstaken; circus
in exodus—the old
ivories tickled.

THOUGHTS ON TWO FISH

I miss the first bout between
sandwich bites—his patient
casting, muffled reeling,
the splash (was there any?)

—and snag awareness
as the angler's net plumps
supple with life. The catch
he extracts is sedate

for a trout, twitchy and silent
in his hands. A monger's cursory
inspection…then release.
Its fusiform length shuttles

downstream, aglint,
content with its lip-piercing from God.

Three minutes before Norm Maclean
lassoes Scaly Acolyte the Second.
This round, I plot the whole affair,
miss no notes of interplay

between species, this Stockholm bond
professed to absurdity
as the magic of the sport (it's not—
it's dopey and dire as a faith

healing, the bellowing ichthys
some traumatized balloon
wet-eyed and puffing for mercy),
and soundless still:

no churning fin,
no river spray.

Loaves and Fishes
blandly handles his prize
(see "Housewife testing cantaloupe
at supermarket")

then plucks free his baptismal
hook, dipping our hostage
back into the flow. It wimples
from the shallows, from his keeping,

its fading soft and bemused;
swimmingly drugged.

Lunch hour ends. I turn for some job
or another, leaving Poseidon
to troll his shore, wondering
with impatience
when my heart might be spooled

through detached, expert grips,
inflicted numinous wounds
that bind and unbind me,
catch and release me,
living mute, marked and changed;

another gasper
for the taking.

EXIT THE LIZARD

Standing still on the kick-off rock we use
to steal height off the rope swing (it's summer,
or fall—its partner-in-tank recently
deceased, so a deliverance feels right),

we watch it breathing there. At first it seems
like it's never moving again—just puffs
those tiny gecko lungs, tempting low birds
to make repast of its reptilic rear,

until we gather its plan—skin becomes
different skin, limey fruit now mottled earth
beneath the fishscale light of arcing pines.
When we want motion more than anything,

it gives—four rubber legs like Viking oars
row its doomed frame into the underbrush.
(Our perspicacious kid brains know by sight
this dew-eyed dragon won't outlive the night.)

Vanished, it leaves its severed tail behind,
a grisly bouquet for us to bury—
but that's fear, that's hope: long abyssal stares,
leaps and self-mutilation. A numb world

to swallow you whole.

TIGER IN PASTEL

My father worked in pastels for a handful of years,
his drawing pads the size of me flipped wide onto

the dining table de-leafed except on holidays. This
was back when his pictures still decorated the hallways

of our house on the dead end road—an etching of
Little Bear, dandy cane in claw, head bucketed,

smirking and marching off the page, and his tiger,
caged in a full moon circle behind bargain bin glass.

The cat he wrought lay in hedonic repose, its yellow
eyes fixed blearily to the right. One paw draped the other

in a gesture of the world-weary, the dismissive
and unenthused; its mane's many folds coiled back

against its shoulders, a pile of talcum softness
beyond which it ceased to exist. Most of my father

was like that: finished before I got there, aloof to the
chagrin of my mother, taciturn about old friends,

how they died in Vietnam (or didn't),
abuser of drink (quietly), alone (always),

the whole of him fleece and forgetting, save that retractable
sardonicism, lying in wait, should his fragile wheelhouse be rocked.

I'd later plan for my own Shere Khan—a fabled third tattoo
on the right wrist, the creature rendered in origami

triangles, shorthand for Miss Earhart's plucky quote:
"...the rest is merely tenacity. The fears are paper tigers..."

That skin's an empty sanctuary; no beasts roam.
Meanwhile, Dad's tiger paced its grave inside the crawl space.

In the forests of some night my father flickered
into coals, used the cinders to render a storybook bear,

then a feline, then quit. By what inexorable infection does
the tiger's blood stir! How I cower at the atavistic symmetry

so many fathers' sons roar against their whole lives
drawing me into reaches of the musty back closet

of the self I never was. There are so few of them left—
young tigers, full fathers—endangered in their prime,

their jungles unexplored by their progeny before they slink
to maul another piece of themselves, all the shadows and

stripes of a life overlapping, reeling from the fires bright
at their tails—mantled briefly, prideless—then folded all away.

TANKA WITH BIRDS

Like the hummingbird
seeks hidden blooms, inspired
at morning's first light,
will I tremble to meet you
in the moment you arrive

***

See the resting crane
at the far end of the lake—
now think on beauty,
how severity and grace
render life untouchable

***

Low moon in the sky—
unreachable as always.
Meanwhile its whiteness
unfurls in the orchids's bloom,
paints the bellies of fat ducks

***

Through gray winter mist
the mourning dove is calling
for its absent half;
Oh young, divided lovers
mend your hearts through bitter song

RONDEAU WITH SHEEP

Down from the fields summer shields in her shade
march a thousand-fold off-white, aubade-
lit bodies, lamb after ewe after lamb
each navigating the traffic jam
twice yearly caused by their shepherds' crusade.
Far be it from we, drivers in sham,
rushed hours, to pass white-knuckled hands
out windows over gauche and bleating babes
down from the fields.

Loud, cotton-soft souls; their Promised Land
near, autumnally this one-note band,
all in its time, will have eaten and laid
bare; winter's mercy a rumor, waylaid,
down from the fields.

THE MEMORY OF DOGS

they flayed and savaged
behind that fence, sister.
dogs cowered and thrashed there
gnawed hope marrow-thin.

ours too was shanghaied, another whelp
pitched like brigantine gold
into pits pooled with glass,
tire rims and teeth. a month at sea
he made landfall at the base of our driveway.

you remember
how we couldn't imagine.

for weeks he palsied under mellow spring heat
shallow breaths at the water bowl
gilded pelt tick-inflamed
and tarred—

our castaway.
we read those ribs topographically.

you, sister, were absent but a night
made pet to uncircumsized dark
stolen by sea hands butter knife sly
operatic and wane as the moon.

your tawny hair medallion bright
the morning you told us,
your posture straight
as sea legs—

our castaway.

think he mangled fellow prisoners?
thieved, sodomized, killed?

sleep-tastes what chain lengths
gored warmth and name from his head?

his eyes hint nothing; all dogs have sad eyes.

you are a dog-lover, sister.
remember the moon of your body
breaking from his brine
your prone, slackened jaw
howling home
from a foreign sleep.

remember for your
amnesic brother to
rattle riggings,
chasten dagger gales,

chapped and indifferent
you may be.

remember somewhere
that fence still stands
his misery dredged far behind it;

to unbury
what burdens you've sunken,
my sister,

and sail on.

VULNERABLE SPECIES

> *"For those groups that have been comprehensively evaluated, the proportion of threatened species can be calculated, but the number...is often uncertain..."*
> — IUCN Red List, Summary Statistics Webpage, December 2019

It's ours—
this devastation reputation,
this tainted taxonomy
at the heart
    of *hominidae*,
cascading,
    resifting,
unfirm ground red-carpet rolling,
the all-too common unsound.

We are no victimless crime:
we are tidal,
    tectonic,
the moon's firm pull
frothing beggar at our feet,
hurriedly, so
    hurriedly
carving the shapes
    of this undoing

from the world's encyclopedias,
generational molds
cast
    and caste,
the only conservation
the conservation of self—

and this,
    our extinction
    of touch.

***

Fossils are touched:
sensuous infinities,
eons' fingers
tumble
      them whole—
rob them
      of rock—
render
      reclamation.
They are no lonely things.

And the soul
      is no petting zoo—
break it, ride it,
breed it anew.
To hell with reluctant pandas—
fuck, fuck
      and be free!

and RSVP
before that second ark buzzes
NO VACANCY,
our bioperversity
sunset-riding
      out of time,

our unicorn heads
beauty-bucking
      in the sand,

and the doves,
      all uncooed
           in the falling.

WOLVERINE IN FOUR FIGURES

1. Roof

Two
hundred
feet in the air,
light not the sun
becomes his vision
from within, the roofing
hammer clenched too tight
releases all at once, that within
light growing to a gossamer smother
he'll live through entirely, no "coming-to,"
a light not Lethe but its opposite once they lay
him convulsing atop the unweathered tiles of their
lake shore job, after he's schlepped down many silver
ladders to the distant earth and the project is built, done for
years, where he'll awaken ram-mad, hate-blind, to the boil-hot spittle
of it all, wholly unsuccumbed, unfallen even once, plunging just for me.

2. Meadow

Some dirt road
or another, hitting
golf balls
into far-off gatherings,
beetle-bored pine.

        His form is admirable:
        little cocky.
        We watch them
        eject
        from our rhythmic
        windmills along
        smooth parabolas,

                strike and shatter bark—
                contact first,
                then the sound becoming.
                We fetch our fodder,
                tee up,
                careen re-collected
                meteor storms

over drowsy flower heads
and prairie dog holes,
birds muting their calls
till it's too damn
hot
to continue.

        Misguided,
        he gifts me clubs
        and their velvety covers:
        memories to closet,
        pawned at later dates.

3. Hospital; Tree

The horrified nurse
gawks at him clutching
the tube two-handed,
pulling its many feet
from his stomach
out his throat:
I can't breathe, Goddamnit!
so there's no more of that
;
Our neighbor
the fireman's
the first to see him
the first to Jaws of Life
him out the car
the first to Flight For Life
him, wear his blood,
the first to call
The Folks now roaring
over winter passes
to cross county lines
to be the first
(should he wake)
thing he sees:
first time a Christmas tree
ever darkened any room.

4. Water Tower

Twelve or thirteen
    drinking beers

feet dangling
    cigarettes passing

their shadows long
    across the gravel

no inklings of golf
    or late night helicopter

flights, all the light
    still without

head still unplated
    (no Frankenstein scars)

leg still bone
    and lacking screws

or a lifetime of hatred
    for the driver, for meds

and falling off roofs
    (tasting air in siblings' minds)

of sobering up
    to choke their frequency

(perversely
    the opposite ensues)

nor the anger
      deep and wild

unwelcomed
      and unbloomed

a fury no words
      can divert

but vocal in the flesh,
      hands shaking

and impotent,
      ready to roundhouse the world

to leap from trees
      and wrestle classmates

a wolverine in spirit
      and school mascot alike, no—

just beers and buds
      under a high mountain sun

whose days they forget
      are numbered.

DEERLY DEPARTED

It's kind of funny because this deer, this buck, gets hit by an ambulance. I'm washing my windshield at the Conoco some August night when I hear a hood crumple inwards and think, *Another fender-bender,* but no, it's a buck barrelled down the Baptist church hill into a vehicle equipped to save lives. Me and two other cars filling up all turn to look and the ambulance lights whirl alive and in their patriotic strobings there lies the broken figure, twitching

at intervals, its neck a goddamned cobra noodling upward, heavenward, The Great Deer Charmer in the Sky calling it home or to pasture or wherever. It shudders and drops from the shattered weight of things, cyclic, insufferable, and the ambulance drivers, they're fine, assessing the token damage, all flashlight sweeps and undertones. And of course Bucky's magic macabre marionette show happens exactly when they look away

(it's kind of funny, really—like that kid making faces behind your friend in class, fingers a theater of secret mocking) and none of us watching fidgets or hollers until a rancher hauling a horse trailer pulls up to the floodlit intersection. He ambles out, one of those no-hipped red-flannelled Farmer Dan varieties, and jaws with the stalled rescue crew, noticing (finally!) Bucky's now five-minute long one-deer interpretative torture dance at the wayside. And the drivers have this

Oh Shit! Moment, their surprise patient lashing on the table, its rack scratching the steaming summer asphault at the crossing, drawing its own forensic body lines, and the trio crouches to Ol' Bucky and Farmer Dan flips open this Real Fucking Knife from his coverall pocket and cuts the beast's throbbing throat like a hunk of cheddar cheese, like a cellist strumming his bow, all ten-thousand hours about it, seasoned and flinchless, a true mercy-killing prodigy.

That's when Bucky's head turns in a way unlike the rest of his spasms, looks into Farmer Dan at that oblique angle of epiphany before deflating like a kiddie pool, and there's this manifest sigh at the pumps like a sickness we're all kicking at the same time, a fever break of the soul before a squad car trundles along and three professionals plus a Farmer Dan heave Ol' Bucky to the apple-blossomed ditch till morning, after which Farmer Dan's knife disappears, and so do we, carry on and carrion, Amen.

TANKA WITH HORSE, BEAVER & ELK

How horses gather
beneath the wide arms of trees
before summer rains
does my heart make its shelter
in your generous embrace

***

It is a pleasure
to fit a plan together,
to follow things through:
What thrill must fill the beaver
lodging in his mighty dam!

***

The cryings of elk
echo through this cold valley,
static under stars;
in this valley hung with stars,
elk cries echo through the cold

THE SPIDER POEM REMEMBERED

It had short lines
throughout,
only two or three stanzas
plus that extra bit
at the end.*

The spider was a pilot
then Quetzalcoatl;
the flies in its web "debris."
An asphyxiation
of alliteration followed—
an anaerobic inch-and-a-half.

I remember looking
up the word *spinnerets*, too.
Grafting it oh so
strategically (like you do).

                      The final thought was offset:
                      no reason.

*(In the white right of here, nearly top
of the page: *Perfection!*
wrote the teacher, his blue
and damning praise.)

MY SISTER'S BREASTS: A CRYPTOZOOLOGICAL INTERVIEW

My sister's breasts are Bigfoot.
    Your response?

We be not Bigfoot, nor his many appelations!
    We exist, for one (for two, if being cheeky).

My sister's breasts are Nessie of the Loch.
    How do you plead?

Still construing Bigfoot:
    You think us hairy? Savage? Elaborate.

My sister's breasts are the Mothman in disguise.
    Any thoughts?

We portend no destruction:
    May Point Pleasant keep its bridges.

My sister's breasts are an ageless mystery.
    Fact or fiction?

We be nine years your senior,
    Immortalized only in that impressionable flash.

My sister's breasts scare children ala Grimm.
    Feeling remorse?

We lost hold of the towel; you were prepubescent.
    Gravity be the culprit, not we.

My sister's breasts summer in the blackest lagoons.
    Can science smoke you out?

We've no need for the trappings of Man:
    Answers be the antipole of fancy.

My sister's breasts haunt the mindwoods of my youth.
   What time's the exorcism?

We refute all misdeeds before The Highest—
   God-fearing domes of flesh, we be!

My sister's breasts are mythology incarnate.
   Will you not laugh with me?

We laugh off the record
   in the rains of sunken valleys
   in the drifts of piercing peaks
   in the marshes forlorn
   and the caves unremembered
   inaccessible, TV-grained,
   a whisper,
   a rumor,
   alone.

...like Bigfoot?
   Not unlike Bigfoot, yes.

My sister's breasts, thank you so much for your time.
   The displeasure, as always, be ours.

PANTOUM WITH RACCOON

The jungle and my mother never met;
so many animals filled her life you'd never know.
For instance, that family of raccoons
she let infest our crawl space for years and years.

You've never known so many animals. Our lives filled
with them, their scratching and their filth
for years and years, our space infested. She let crawl
all of God's fuzzy creatures, some birds, never bugs,

and their scratching, their filth...With them
she played a minor savior brimming with food
for all of God's fuzzy creatures (never bugs). Some hummingbirds
she fed flew bloated from her excess of nectar.

Fed to the brim, minorly she played their savior,
their flightpaths drunken and dizzied
from her *nectar excessif*. She fled few bloated
mammals from our property (save the biggest carnivores),

their paths and their flights dizzy and drunk
off her kindness. Those that stayed learned—
save the biggest carnivores—mammals from our property
were rarely evicted, and should that day come they'd be old

and learned. Off her kindness, those that stayed
took everything, ate everything and more;
come eviction day, that rarity, they'd be old. And should
any houseguest bite her hand too long or too hard,

take everything, eat everything and more—
"nuisance" or "pest" never shadowed her lips.
Too long and too hard her houseguests bit her hand?
That day never came; her bounty was her curse.

My mother and the jungle never met.
Her lips never shadowed with "nuisance" or "pest."
That day never came; her bounty was her curse.
Every houseguest bit her hand too long and too hard,
ate everything, took everything and more.
That family of raccoons, for instance.

SMILODON SONG

> "*For four decades, guests have been greeted by the saber-tooth cat, which roars when money is placed in its mouth! The cat collects as much as $10,000 a year...*"
> —Denver Museum of Nature & Science Archive Website

> "*Denver museum's saber-tooth cat updated with new roars*"
> —Denver Post headline, June 1, 2019

Forty-year feline, bust most beloved,
long-throated eater of children's spare coins,
rejoice! Your jaws and fangs, plaster reborn,
render throngs of Modern Man exultant!

O Pleistocene jukebox, doorman declawed,
your cistern engorged by coppers and zincs
of a thousand-and-one urban field trips,
persist! May your slight repertoire of roars,

long of tooth, redouble its digital
thrills into epochs undawned! New B-sides
for hairball and housecat mewl now append
old soundbytes, chimerical reduxxes,

their echoes turning heads forevermore!
Give thanks for this, your resurrected lot,
to stir and elate ambling apes upright
traversing your floorwaxed domain! Harken,

creature deceased and mute to bygone ears,
bellowing over linoleum plains
your birthright, that pre-recorded terror,
to tribes of spearless bipeds by the score,

their halls and their rafters booming your claim,
not taxidermy nor mascot nor prop—
just Saber, eternal, yowling at fee,
extinct to no heart of this Mile-High City!

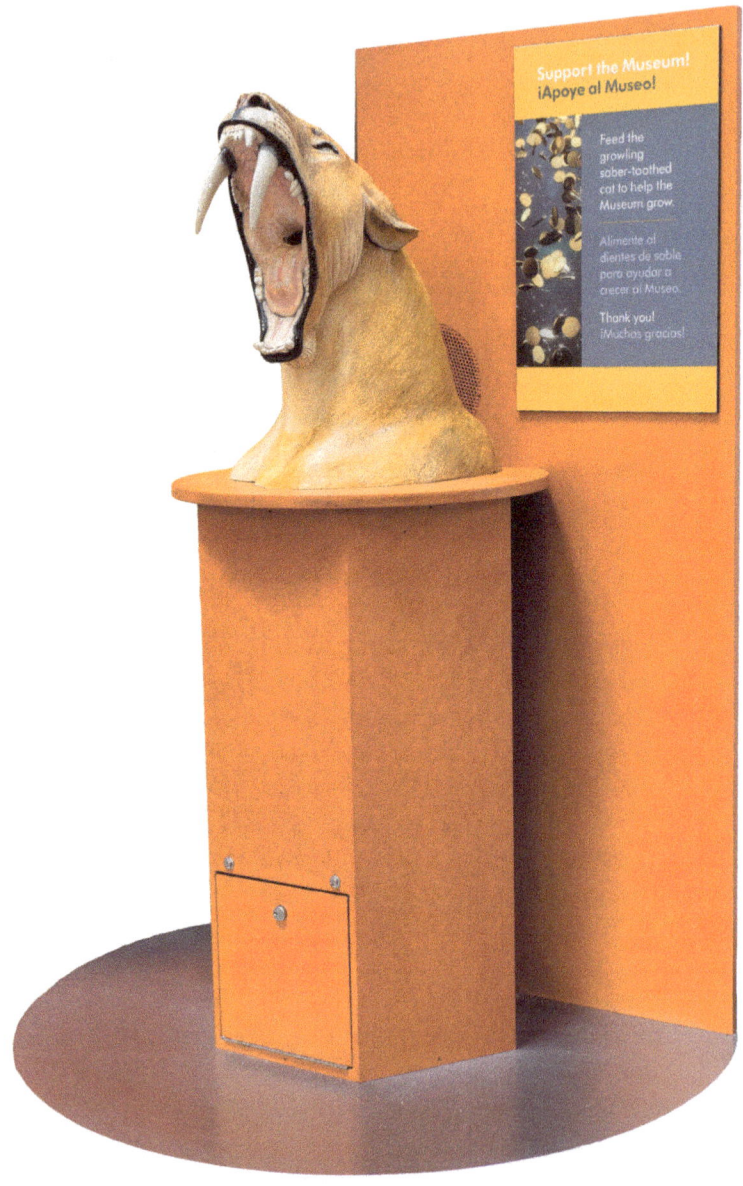

Garrett Ray Harriman is a writer and poet living in southwest Colorado. His work has appeared in *Atlas Poetica, Toasted Cheese, Kestrel,* and other publications. His poem "Snake in the Grass" was a semi-finalist in *Naugatuck River Review*'s 11th Narrative Poetry Contest guest judged by poet Lauren K. Alleyne. When not writing he can be found hiking, playing saxophone, and learning languages. Please follow him on Twitter (@Inadversent) or visit InadversentPoetry.com.

www.ingramcontent.com/pod-product-compliance
Lightning Source LLC
Chambersburg PA
CBHW050821090426
42737CB00022B/3471